Here Comes

BONK!

A FAWCETT CREST BOOK

Fawcett Publications, Inc., Greenwich, Conn.

Member of American Book Publishers Council, Inc.

Charlie Brown!

Selected Cartoons from
GOOD 'OL CHARLIE BROWN
Vol. II

by Charles M. Schulz

HERE COMES CHARLIE BROWN

This book, prepared especially for Fawcett Publications, Inc., comprises the second half of GOOD OL' CHARLIE BROWN, and is reprinted by arrangement with Holt, Rinehart and Winston, Inc.

Thirteenth Fawcett Crest printing, January 1968

Published by Fawcett World Library, 67 West 44th Street, New York, New York 10036. Printed in the United States of America

ZOOM!

NOW, YOU CUT THAT OUT!

SCHULZ

I HAVE A TUNE THAT KEEPS RUNNING THROUGH MY MIND..
THAT'S STRANGE.. I HAVE, TOO, CHARLIE BROWN..
IT'S THAT PART IN BRAHMS' SECOND WHERE THE PIANO GOES 'DEEDLE DEEDLE DEEDLE..'
AND THEN THE ORCHESTRA FOLLOWS WITH 'BAHM BAAHM **BAHM BAHM** BEEDLE..'
AND THEN THE PIANO COMES IN AGAIN, '**DUM DUM DUM** DLUM TDLUM TLUM...' AND..
SIGH

YOU KNOW THE KIND OF PERSON I MEAN..THEY'RE SORT OF....
WELL, TAKE CHARLIE BROWN,HERE, HE'S A PERFECT EXAMPLE...
?
OH, YES, NOW I KNOW **EXACTLY** WHAT YOU MEAN..
SIGH